Yolanda's
Blueberry Cookbook

Best Wishes
Yolanda Lodi

Also by Yolanda Lodi

———

Yolanda's Cranberry Country Recipes

Yolanda's Hand-Me-Down Recipes

Yolanda's Blueberry Cookbook

Rock Village Publishing
Middleborough MA

Yolanda's Blueberry Cookbook
Copyright © 2005 by Yolanda Lodi

Typography and cover by Ruth Brown

ISBN 0-9766356-1-5

Rock Village Publishing
41 Walnut Street
Middleborough MA 02346
(508) 946-4738

Dedication

To my husband,
Ed,
who loves to eat.

"We have *such* good times together."

CONTENTS

Introduction

Breakfast & Brunch

Soup & Fruit Salads

Chicken

Cakes & Cheesecake

Contents

Cobblers & Crisps

Pies

Cookies & Sweets

Special Feature

"Kristine's Culinary Creations"

Yolanda's
Blueberry Cookbook

Introduction

A Peek at What's Inside

With one or two exceptions, the recipes in *Yolanda's Blueberry Cookbook* are easy to prepare. For example, Nancy's Chilled Blueberry Soup requires virtually no cooking and tastes great on a hot summer day. Plan to make it two hours before serving, since the soup needs to chill an hour and a half. If it is left to chill longer or if any is left over, serve it as a mousse for dessert. But I doubt if there will be leftovers! Another simple cold recipe is Blueberry Yogurt Pie; even a child could put it together. This pie needs four hours in the freezer and 30 minutes at room temperature before serving.

A couple of recipes that require no baking and are best made with fresh blueberries are Sweet B&B Pie and Barbara's No-Bake Pie. (Incidentally, the B&B refers to the blueberries and bananas, not to a bed and breakfast.) This pie will satisfy anyone's sweet tooth. Barbara's pie tastes like a cheesecake with loads of blueberries. Both these as well as the yogurt pie use baked graham shells that supermarkets sell ready to fill. Another recipe that is best with fresh blueberries is Sally's Open Blueberry Pie (though the bottom crust needs baking).

For those who love fresh fruit in the summertime—and who doesn't?—there's Blueberry Ambrosia made with blueberries, pineapple and grapes. This is strictly for the 21-and-up crowd. The fruit marinates in wine for two to three hours. The under-21 crowd or the young-at-heart can indulge in Fruit Dressing, spooned over fresh blueberries and other fruits. "I usually double the recipe since it's a big hit," states Ann Marashio who gave me the recipe.

For those Fourth of July celebrations make Fudge for the Fourth. The red color of dried cranberries along with dried blueberries mixed with white chocolate give, not only a sparkling effect, but also a sweet and tart taste. Place the pieces on a dark blue plate and bring it to your next party.

I find that wild dried blueberries taste better as an ingredient than eaten plain. The next three recipes use dried wild blueberries. One of my favorites is Blueberry Butter Cookies. They melt in your mouth with a pleasant blueberry taste and are fun to make. I feel like a child again when shaping small amounts of dough to form a cookie. The dried blueberries in Kisses for Kids add a special flavor to the sweetness of the meringue. For a more healthful treat, make Blueberry Teacakes. Besides the dried blueberries, some of the other ingredients are whole-wheat flour, applesauce, skim milk, and olive oil. There's only one-quarter cup of sugar in the recipe. These little teacakes offer loads of blueberry flavor. Everyone who's tried them loves them.

For healthful recipes using fresh blueberries, try Whole-Wheat Blueberry Muffins and Blueberry Corn Muffins. The names say it all. Not only are they good, but they are tasty. The best in the muffins category is Helen's Blueberry Muffins. The recipe calls for sprinkled sugar over the top of the batter before baking. An added bonus is the "you can't bottle it" baking smell that fills the house while the muffins are baking and lingers many hours afterwards.

Other great breakfast treats are Blueberry Corn Bread, Blueberry Nut Bread, Blueberry Lemon Bread, and Donna's Blueberry Scones. Both the lemon bread, containing juice and zest, and the scones, with their lemon glaze, have a pleasing lemon taste. Delicious!

Donna Truran, who owns The Blueberry Patch in East Wareham, shared her cake recipe along with her scones. "Each week I have a new recipe for our 'Pick Your Own' customers. These two are the ones most asked for," says Donna.

Other recipes that have gotten rave reviews from my friends are John's Blueberry Cake, Anna's Blueberry Cream Cheese Coffeecake, and Jenny's Blueberry Squares; the latter has been in Jenny's family for years.

While sampling one of my blueberry creations, Kathy Perry said, "My godson, Chris, loves blueberries and has a great cobbler that our family always looks forward to." It's easy to make and delicious. The individual servings make for an elegant presentation.

Marilyn's Blueberry Cobbler is also easy to throw together. The only dish used in preparing it is the baking dish. From beginning to end this recipe takes only a half hour.

Blueberry Gobbler takes some time to prepare but is worth the wait, especially for those who love loads of blueberries. Everyone will be sure to *gobble* this one up.

Whenever my husband and I visit our friend Dorthy Massey, we can look forward to something good baking in the oven. On a recent visit, after chitchatting a while, I asked, "What smells so good?"

"Blueberry something," she said.

"Blueberry 'something'?"

"Yes. Instead of making pie crust I make dough similar to pie crust and spoon it over the fruit."

Ed and I not only enjoyed Dorthy's Blueberry "Something", but also, as usual, our visit. She always has interesting stories to share. Before we left, I asked Dorthy for the recipe. As she gave it to me, she mentioned that she sometimes throws a few raw cranberries in for added tart flavor. I thought, "She's like me; she loves to experiment." I wonder what's cooking at her house today?

Two favorite berries come together in Ted Murphy's Cranberry and Blueberry Chocolate Pie. Ted is the chef at the Mountaineer Inn, located at the base of Mount Snow in West Dover, Vermont. Last summer Ed and I spent a pleasant week attending an Elderhostel program sponsored by Innkeepers Royal and Ned Wilson. Each morning we looked forward to breakfast and selecting our dinner entrée. Always listed on the menu was that evening's dessert. When I read Cranberry and Blueberry Chocolate Pie, I just had to get the recipe. After checking with Royal, I approached Ted, who graciously explained how he makes his pie. Like a true chef, he doesn't use precise measurements. After converting Ted's "measurements" to exact ones, I made the pie and served it for dessert last Christmas. Everyone not only enjoyed Ted's pie, but the stories of our memorable week in the mountains of Vermont as well.

In Vermont we also reconnected with Rita Domian, whom we hadn't seen in over ten years and, who, coincidently, was attending the same program. Her *joie de vivre* and humor added a special touch throughout the week. Shortly after arriving home I received her blueberry pierogi recipe in the mail. This was a challenge. After making the dough, I tried rolling out a third of it. Not having enough muscle, I couldn't get the dough thin enough. Then I remembered my pasta machine. With the disk at maximum setting, I fed a slice of dough through the rollers. I repeated the process, reducing the setting each time, ending with the tightest setting and the equivalent of rolled out thin dough. Success! The rest fell into place.

As do all the rest of these tasty blueberry creations. ☺

Breakfast & Brunch

Blueberry Corn Bread

  2 cups all-purpose flour
  1 cup yellow cornmeal
 ¾ cup sugar
  1 Tbsp. baking powder
 ½ tsp. salt
  1 cup blueberries
  2 large eggs
1½ cups skim milk
  1 Tbsp. butter, melted

Preheat oven to 400 degrees.

Grease and flour a 13- x 9- x 2-inch pan.

In a large bowl sift together flour, cornmeal, sugar, baking powder, and salt. Stir in blueberries.

In a medium-size bowl whisk eggs. Add milk and melted butter. Whisk until foamy. Add to the large bowl. Mix with a spoon until the dry ingredients are moistened.

Pour into greased and floured pan.

Bake at 400 degrees for 25 to 30 minutes or until toothpick inserted in center comes out clean.

Cool on a wire rack.

Makes 12 to 15 servings.

Blueberry Lemon Bread

3 cups all-purpose flour
1 cup sugar
4 tsp. baking powder
½ tsp. salt
1 large egg
1½ cups skim milk
2 Tbsp. olive oil
1 tsp. lemon juice
1½ cups blueberries, floured (toss in a small amount of flour until all the berries are coated)
4 tsp. grated lemon zest

Preheat oven to 350 degrees.

Grease and flour a 9- x 5- x 3-inch loaf pan.

In a large bowl combine flour, sugar, baking powder, and salt. Mix with a spoon.

In a medium-size bowl whisk egg. Add milk, olive oil, and lemon juice. Whisk until foamy.

Add to dry ingredients. Mix to form a batter. Fold in floured blueberries and lemon zest.

Spread into greased and floured loaf pan.

Bake at 350 degrees for at least one hour. Test by inserting toothpick in center. Ready when pick comes out with moist crumbs.

Cool on a wire rack for 15 minutes. Then remove from pan.

Makes 1 loaf.

Blueberry Nut Bread

  1 cup all-purpose flour
  ½ cup whole-wheat flour
  ½ cup sugar
1½ tsp. baking powder
  ¼ tsp. baking soda
  ¼ tsp. ground nutmeg
  ⅛ tsp. salt
  1 large egg
  ½ cup applesauce
  2 Tbsp. olive oil
  1 cup blueberries, floured (toss in a small amount of flour until all the berries are coated)
  ¼ cup chopped walnuts

Preheat oven to 350 degrees.

Grease and flour a 9- x 5- x 3-inch loaf pan.

In a large bowl combine flours, sugar, baking powder, baking soda, nutmeg, and salt. Mix with a spoon.

In a small bowl beat egg until foamy. Add applesauce and olive oil. Mix at low speed until well blended. Add to the large bowl and mix with a spoon until the dry ingredients are moistened.

Fold in floured blueberries and chopped walnuts.

Spread into greased and floured loaf pan.

Bake at 350 degrees for 40 minutes or until toothpick inserted in center comes out clean.

Cool on a wire rack for 15 minutes. Then remove from pan.

Makes 1 loaf.

Anna's Blueberry Cream Cheese Coffeecake

½ cup (1 stick) margarine, softened
1¼ cups sugar
2 eggs
2¼ cups all-purpose flour
1 Tbsp. baking powder
1 cup skim milk
1 container (8 oz.) whipped cream cheese
1 Tbsp. lemon juice
½ tsp. almond extract
2 cups blueberries, floured (toss in a small amount of flour until all the berries are coated)

Topping
¼ cup sugar
¼ cup all-purpose flour
2 Tbsp. (¼ stick) margarine, cut into small pieces
Ground cinnamon (to sprinkle over top)
Sugar (to sprinkle over top)

Preheat oven to 350 degrees.

Grease and flour a 13- x 9- x 2-inch pan.

In a large bowl, with mixer at low speed, cream margarine and sugar until smooth and fluffy. Add eggs. Beat until well blended.

In a separate bowl combine flour and baking powder.

With mixer at medium speed, add flour mixture to large bowl, alternately with milk, until blended.

Add cream cheese, lemon juice, and almond extract. Blend well by hand.

Fold in floured blueberries.

Pour batter into greased and floured pan.

Topping
In a small bowl mix sugar, flour, and margarine until crumbly. Sprinkle over batter. Then sprinkle some cinnamon and sugar.

Bake at 350 degrees for 55 to 60 minutes or until toothpick inserted in center comes out clean.

Makes 12 servings.

Blueberry Breakfast Cakes

4   large eggs
1   cup skim milk
1   cup all-purpose flour
2   Tbsp. sugar
½   tsp. vanilla extract
2   Tbsp. (¼ stick) butter
1   cup blueberries
    Warm maple syrup

Two 8-inch glass pie plates

Preheat oven to 425 degrees.

In a large bowl beat eggs, milk, flour, sugar, and vanilla until well blended.

Place one Tbsp. butter in each pie plate and place in oven until butter melts.

Remove from oven. Carefully tilt each pie plate to coat bottom with melted butter.

Pour one-half of the batter into each of the pie plates. Evenly arrange blueberries on top of batter.

Bake at 425 degrees for about 15 minutes or until golden brown.

Transfer each cake to a serving plate.

Serve immediately with warm maple syrup.

Makes 2 to 4 servings.

Blueberry Teacakes

1	cup all-purpose flour
¾	cup whole-wheat flour
¼	cup sugar
1	Tbsp. baking powder
¼	tsp. salt
¾	cup applesauce
¼	cup skim milk
¼	cup olive oil
1	cup dried wild blueberries

Preheat oven to 400 degrees.

Grease twelve-2½-inch-muffin-cup pan well with butter.

In a large bowl sift together flours, sugar, baking powder, and salt.

Form a well in the center of the bowl.

Add applesauce, milk, and olive oil. Mix with a spoon until the dry ingredients are moistened.

Fold in dried wild blueberries.

Spoon batter into muffin pan.

Bake at 400 degrees for 20 minutes or until toothpick inserted in center comes out clean.

Makes 12 teacakes.

Blueberry Corn Muffins

1	cup all-purpose flour
1	cup yellow cornmeal
¼	cup sugar
1½	Tbsp. baking powder
½	tsp. salt
1	cup blueberries
1	large egg
1	cup skim milk
2	Tbsp. (¼ stick) butter, melted

Preheat oven to 400 degrees.

Grease twelve-2½-inch-muffin-cup pan well with butter, including the top surface of pan.

In a large bowl sift together flour, cornmeal, sugar, baking powder, and salt. Stir in blueberries.

In a medium-size bowl whisk egg. Add milk and melted butter. Whisk until foamy. Add to the large bowl. Mix with a spoon until the dry ingredients are moistened.

Spoon batter into muffin cups.

Bake at 400 degrees for 20 minutes or until toothpick inserted in center comes out clean.

Makes 12 muffins.

Helen's Blueberry Muffins

½ cup (1 stick) butter, softened
1¼ cups sugar
2 eggs
2 cups all-purpose flour
2 tsp. baking powder
½ tsp. salt
½ cup milk
2 cups blueberries, floured (toss in a small amount of flour until all the berries are coated)
2 tsp. sugar (to sprinkle over top of muffins)

Preheat oven to 400 degrees.

Grease twelve-2½-inch-muffin-cup pan well with butter, including the top surface of pan.

In a large bowl, with mixer at low speed, cream butter and sugar until smooth and fluffy. Add one egg at a time, making sure batter continues to be fluffy.

In a separate bowl sift together flour, baking powder, and salt.

With mixer at medium speed, add sifted ingredients to large bowl, alternately with milk, until blended.

Fold in floured blueberries.

Spoon batter into muffin cups. Sprinkle sugar on top.

Bake at 400 degrees for the **first 10** minutes.

Lower oven temperature to 375 degrees. Bake an **additional** 25 to 30 minutes.

Makes 12 muffins.

Whole-Wheat Blueberry Muffins

- 1 cup whole-wheat flour
- 1 cup all-purpose flour
- ¼ cup sugar
- 1 Tbsp. baking powder
- ¼ tsp. salt
- 1 large egg
- 1 cup skim milk
- ¼ cup olive oil
- 1 cup blueberries, floured (toss in a small amount of flour until all the berries are coated)
- ½ cup chopped walnuts

Preheat oven to 425 degrees.

Grease twelve-2½-inch-muffin-cup pan well with butter, including the top surface of pan.

In a large bowl combine flours, sugar, baking powder, and salt. Mix with a spoon.

In a medium-size bowl whisk egg. Then add milk and olive oil. Whisk until foamy.

Add to the large bowl. Mix with a spoon until the dry ingredients are moistened.

Fold in floured blueberries and chopped walnuts.

Spoon batter into muffin pan.

Bake at 425 degrees for 20 minutes or until toothpick inserted in center comes out clean.

Makes 12 muffins.

Donna's Blueberry Scones

2 cups all-purpose flour
⅓ cup sugar
2 tsp. baking powder
½ tsp. baking soda
¼ tsp. salt
¼ cup (½ stick) margarine, melted
1 container (8 oz.) lemon or vanilla yogurt
1 egg, lightly beaten
1 tsp. grated lemon zest
1 cup blueberries

Glaze
½ cup confectioners' sugar
1 Tbsp. lemon juice
½ tsp. grated lemon zest

Preheat oven to 400 degrees.

Grease baking sheet.

In a large bowl combine flour, sugar, baking powder, baking soda, and salt.

In a separate bowl mix melted margarine, yogurt, egg, and lemon zest.

Add to dry ingredients and stir until just moistened. Batter will be stiff and somewhat lumpy.

Fold in blueberries.

Drop batter one spoonful at a time onto greased baking sheet.

Bake at 400 degrees for 15 to 18 minutes or until lightly browned.

Glaze
In a small bowl mix the glaze ingredients. Let stand while scones are baking.

Remove scones from oven.

Spread glaze on scones while still warm.

Makes 9 to 12 scones.

Jenny's Blueberry Squares

1 cup (2 sticks) butter, softened
1 cup sugar
2 eggs
1 tsp. vanilla extract
2 cups all-purpose flour
1 cup chopped walnuts
1 can (21 oz.) blueberry pie filling

Preheat oven to 350 degrees.

Grease a 13- x 9- x 2-inch pan.

In a large bowl, with mixer at low speed, cream butter, sugar, eggs, and vanilla. Add flour. Mix at medium speed until well blended.

Fold in chopped walnuts.

Spread *half* of the dough in greased pan. Evenly spoon pie filling over dough. Using a teaspoon, drop (here and there) remaining dough on top of the pie filling.

Bake on lower rack at 350 degrees for the **first 30** minutes.

Then move pan to middle rack. Bake an **additional** 30 minutes.

Cool on a wire rack.

Makes 12 squares.

Rita's Blueberry Pierogi

Dough
2¼ to 2½ cups all-purpose flour
½ tsp. salt
1 small egg
½ cup hot water (not boiling)
1 to 2 Tbsp. olive oil

Filling
4 cups blueberries, washed and drained
1 tsp. potato starch

Cooking the Pierogi
1 large pot of water
1 Tbsp. olive oil

Topping
Granulated sugar or confectioners' sugar
(to sprinkle over top)

Making the Dough
Sift flour onto a wooden board. Sprinkle salt over flour.

Make a well in the center and add egg. Using a knife, mix the outlying flour into the egg.

Gradually add hot water in a thin stream and work mixture by hand into a dough, gradually working in the olive oil. Knead well until dough is smooth and elastic, and no longer sticks to hand.

Form 3 balls of dough. Cover with a warm bowl (so it doesn't dry out) until ready to use.

Preparing the Filling
Dust blueberries with potato starch.

Forming the Pierogi
On a lightly floured board, roll out thin one-third of the dough, leaving the remaining dough under the warm bowl.

Using a biscuit cutter (or a drinking glass), cut dough into 3-inch round pieces.

Place a spoonful of filling just off center on each dough round. Fold over. Pinch edges of dough together firmly to seal in the filling.

Cooking the Pierogi
Bring the water and oil to a rapid boil.

Continued...

Rita's Blueberry Pierogi...continued

Drop a dozen filled pierogi into the boiling water.

Return water to a rapid boil. Cook uncovered, stirring gently, for 4 to 5 minutes.

Carefully remove from pan with perforated spoon. Drain on paper towels.

Sprinkle with either granulated sugar or confectioners' sugar.

Serve with sour cream (or yogurt) or heavy sweet cream.

Makes 5 to 6 dozen pierogi.

Soup & Fruit Salads

Nancy's Chilled Blueberry Soup

1	can (15 oz.) blueberries, packed in light syrup
1½	tsp. plain gelatin
1	cup plain yogurt
½	cup orange juice
⅓	cup heavy cream
1½	Tbsp. honey
¼	tsp. ground cinnamon
	Ground nutmeg to taste

Strain blueberries. Reserve **all** blueberry juice.

Pour blueberry juice into a measuring cup to the 1/3 mark. Stir in gelatin until dissolved.

Pour gelatin mixture into a small saucepan. Heat to boiling point.

Remove from heat. Set aside.

In a large bowl, with mixer at low speed, mix yogurt, orange juice, heavy cream, honey, and cinnamon, until blended.

Stir in gelatin mixture, blueberries, and remaining blueberry juice.

Cover and chill until thickened (at least 1½ hours).

Sprinkle ground nutmeg to taste.

Makes 6 to 8 servings.

Blueberry Ambrosia

1 cup blueberries
1 cup fresh pineapple, cut in small pieces
1 cup green seedless grapes, halved
½ cup White Zinfandel
½ cup shredded coconut

In a clear glass bowl combine all ingredients **except** shredded coconut.

Cover bowl tightly with plastic wrap and refrigerate 2 to 3 hours. Serve chilled.

When ready to serve, sprinkle shredded coconut over the top.

Makes 4 servings.

Fruit Dressing

Spoon over fresh blueberries.

> 1 package (8 oz.) cream cheese, softened
> 1 jar (7½ oz.) Marshmallow Fluff®
> ¼ cup orange juice
> Dash ground ginger

In a large bowl, with mixer at medium speed, blend cream cheese and fluff until smooth and fluffy.

Add orange juice and ginger. Continue with mixer at medium speed until mixture is smooth and well blended.

Makes about 2 cups.

Ann Marashio says:

Credit has to go to my husband's aunt, Vivianne Lemaire from Fairhaven, Massachusetts, an incredible cook who recently passed away. She used to make this recipe and bring it with fresh fruit to our summer cookouts. I'd ask her, "What's in it?" But she refused to tell me until I tried it, fearing that, like many people, I'd be turned off by the fluff. After numerous attempts to try to find out what was in it, I finally gave in and tried it. I immediately became hooked! I started serving it to my family and friends and, believe me, many times there is none left over, no matter how much I make.

I usually double the recipe since it's a big hit.

Chicken

"Am I Blue?" Chicken

2 lbs. chicken breasts, boneless and
skinless, cut in half and flattened
¼ cup bread crumbs

Sauce
1 cup blueberries
1 cup red onion, chopped
½ cup water
2 Tbsp. (¼ stick) butter
1 tsp. cornstarch
1 Tbsp. cold water
⅛ tsp. salt
⅛ tsp. black pepper

Preheat oven to 400 degrees.

Butter an oven-proof glass dish large enough to contain the chicken breasts.

In a saucepan combine blueberries, red onion, and water. Bring to a full boil. Reduce heat to medium.

Stir in butter until melted. Dilute cornstarch in cold water. Add to the saucepan along with salt and pepper. Cook over low heat, stirring constantly, until mixture begins to thicken.

Remove from stove and set aside.

Coat both sides of the chicken pieces with bread crumbs. Place them in buttered dish.

Pour sauce over chicken. Cover with aluminum foil.

Bake at 400 degrees for 30 minutes.

Serve over rice.

Makes 4 servings.

Cakes & Cheesecake

"The Blueberry Patch" Cake

- 1 cup shortening
- 1½ cups sugar
- 2 tsp. vanilla extract
- 4 eggs, separated
- 3 cups all-purpose flour
- 2 tsp. baking powder
- ½ tsp. ground ginger
- ½ tsp. salt
- ⅔ cup milk
- ½ cup sugar
- 3 cups blueberries

Glaze
- Juice from one lemon
- ½ tsp. grated lemon zest
- ½ cup sugar

Preheat oven to 350 degrees.

Grease a 13- x 9- x 2-inch pan.

In a large bowl, with mixer at low speed, cream shortening and sugar. Add vanilla and egg yolks. Beat until light and fluffy.

In a separate bowl mix flour, baking powder, ginger, and salt.

With mixer at medium speed, add dry ingredients to creamed mixture, alternately with milk, until well blended.

Beat egg whites until stiff. Gradually add sugar, beating after each addition, so egg whites remain stiff. Fold into batter.

Fold in blueberries.

Pour into greased pan.

Bake at 350 degrees for 50 minutes or until cake tests done.

In a small bowl mix the glaze ingredients. Let stand while cake is baking.

Remove cake from oven. While cake is still hot, brush glaze over top of cake with a pastry brush (or spoon).

Makes 12 servings.

Blueberry Flat Cake

½ cup (1 stick) butter
1 cup all-purpose flour
1 cup sugar
1 tsp. baking powder
1 cup skim milk
1 egg, beaten with a fork
1 tsp. vanilla extract
2 cups blueberries

CAKES & CHEESECAKE

Preheat oven to 350 degrees.

Melt butter in a 13- x 9- x 2-inch glass oven-proof baking dish. Tilt to coat sides.

In a large bowl combine flour, sugar, and baking powder. With a spoon stir in milk, egg, and vanilla until well blended.

Pour into baking dish containing melted butter. Evenly arrange blueberries over top.

Bake at 350 degrees for 30 to 35 minutes or until toothpick inserted in center comes out clean and edges are golden brown.

Cool on a wire rack.

Makes 8 to 10 servings.

Blueberry Upside-Down Cake

    2   cups blueberries
    1   cup sugar, divided
    ½   cup (1 stick) butter, softened
    1   large egg
    1   tsp. vanilla extract
    2   cups all-purpose flour
    1   Tbsp. baking powder
    ⅛   tsp. salt
    1   cup skim milk

Preheat oven to 350 degrees.

Generously butter a 9-inch square baking pan.

Line bottom of buttered baking pan with blueberries. Sprinkle one-half cup of sugar over blueberries. Set aside.

In a large bowl, with mixer at low speed, cream butter and remaining one-half cup of sugar. Add egg and vanilla. Beat until light and fluffy.

In a separate bowl sift together flour, baking powder, and salt.

With mixer at medium speed, add sifted ingredients to creamed mixture, alternately with milk, until well blended.

Spread batter evenly over blueberries.

Bake at 350 degrees for about 45 minutes until top is browned. Test by inserting toothpick in center. Ready when pick comes out with moist crumbs.

Cool in pan on a wire rack for 5 minutes before inverting cake onto serving plate.

Makes 9 servings.

Blueberry Yogurt Cake

1 cup (2 sticks) butter, softened
1 cup brown sugar
1 large egg
1 tsp. vanilla extract
2 cups all-purpose flour
1 tsp. baking soda
½ tsp. baking powder
⅛ tsp. salt
1 container (8 oz.) vanilla yogurt
1 cup blueberries, floured (toss in a small amount of flour until all the berries are coated)
Confectioners' sugar (to sprinkle over top)

Preheat oven to 350 degrees.

Grease and flour a 9-inch square baking pan.

In a large bowl, with mixer at low speed, cream butter and brown sugar. Beat in egg and vanilla until light and fluffy.

In a separate bowl combine flour, baking soda, baking powder, and salt.

Add dry ingredients to creamed mixture along with yogurt. Mix with a spoon until the dry ingredients are moistened.

Fold in floured blueberries.

Spread batter into greased and floured baking pan.

Bake at 350 degrees for 45 minutes or until toothpick inserted in center comes out clean.

Cool on a wire rack.

Sprinkle with confectioners' sugar.

Makes 9 servings.

John's Blueberry Cake

1¾ cups *plus* 2 Tbsp. sugar
½ cup *plus* 2 Tbsp. shortening
2 large eggs
3 cups all-purpose flour
2½ tsp. baking powder
1 tsp. salt
1¼ cups milk
1½ tsp. vanilla extract
2 cups blueberries, washed and drained

Preheat oven to 375 degrees.

Grease and flour a 13- x 9- x 2-inch pan.

In a large bowl, with mixer at low speed, cream sugar and shortening. Beat in eggs until light and fluffy.

In a separate bowl combine flour, baking powder, and salt. Set aside ¼ **cup** of flour mixture for later (to coat the berries).

Pour milk into a measuring cup. Stir in vanilla.

With mixer at medium speed, add flour mixture to shortening mixture, alternately with milk, until blended. Set aside.

Toss blueberries in ¼ **cup** flour mixture.

Fold floured blueberries, along with any remaining flour mixture, into batter.

Pour batter into greased and floured pan.

Bake at 375 degrees for 45 to 60 minutes.

Makes 12 servings.

Blueberry Country Cheesecake

Crust
- 1¼ cups graham cracker crumbs
  (11 rectangular graham crackers)
- 4 Tbsp. (½ stick) butter, melted
- 1 Tbsp. sugar

Filling
- 3 packages (8 oz. each) cream cheese, softened
- ¾ cup sugar
- 1 Tbsp. all-purpose flour
- 1½ tsp. vanilla extract
- 3 large eggs
- 1 egg yolk
- ¼ cup skim milk

Topping
- 2 cups fresh blueberries, divided
- ½ cup sugar
- ¼ cup water
- 1 Tbsp. lemon juice
- 1 Tbsp. cornstarch
- ⅛ tsp. salt
- 1 tsp. butter

Preheat oven to 375 degrees.

Crust
Prepare food processor for chopping.

Place crust ingredients in work bowl. Pulse until mixture is crumbs.

Using your fingers, press the buttered crumbs evenly and firmly onto the bottom and up the sides of an 8½-inch springform pan.

Bake at 375 degrees for 10 minutes.

Cool on a wire rack.

Lower oven temperature to 300 degrees.

Filling
In a large bowl, with mixer at medium speed, beat cream cheese and sugar until mixture is smooth and fluffy. Beat in flour and vanilla until combined.

Reduce speed to low. Add one egg at a time, including extra yolk, beating after each addition. Beat in milk until blended.

Pour batter into springform pan.

Bake at 300 degrees for 55 to 60 minutes until lightly golden and the area three inches from the center is slightly wet.

Blueberry Country Cheesecake...continued

Cool completely on a wire rack before refrigerating overnight.

Topping
In a small saucepan combine **one cup** blueberries, sugar, water, lemon juice, cornstarch, and salt.

Cook and stir over medium-high heat until mixture begins to boil. Continue to stir for an additional minute until mixture comes to a full boil.

Remove from heat.

Stir in butter.

Cool completely.

Cover and refrigerate overnight.

The next day

Combine the remaining one cup of blueberries to the cold, cooked berries.

Place cheesecake on a serving plate. Remove side of springform pan.

Garnish cheesecake with blueberry topping.

Makes 12 servings.

Note: This blueberry topping makes a delicious topping for ice cream.

Cobblers & Crisps

Chris's Blueberry Cobbler

    3   Tbsp. butter
    2   cups fresh blueberries
    2   Tbsp. water
    1   Tbsp. grated lemon zest
    3   Tbsp. cornstarch
    ¾   cup sugar

    Six 6-10 oz. ramekins

Topping
    1   cup all-purpose flour
    ¾   cup sugar
    1   tsp. baking powder
    ½   tsp. salt
    1   cup milk
    1   large egg
    ¼   cup vegetable shortening
    1   tsp. vanilla extract

Preheat oven to 350 degrees.

In a medium saucepan melt butter. Stir in blueberries, water, and lemon zest.

Add cornstarch and sugar. Cook over medium heat, stirring constantly, until slightly thickened, 6 to 8 minutes.

Pour even amounts into each ramekin. Let stand while making topping.

Topping
Into a mixing bowl sift flour, sugar, baking powder, and salt. Add milk, egg, shortening, and vanilla. Beat at medium speed for 2 to 3 minutes.

Pour topping into each ramekin containing the cooked blueberries.

Place the filled ramekins on a baking sheet.

Bake at 350 degrees for about 35 to 40 minutes.

Add a scoop of vanilla ice cream before serving.

Makes 6 servings.

Marilyn's Blueberry Cobbler

- 3   cups fresh blueberries, or 1 package (12 oz.) frozen blueberries, thawed
- ½   cup sugar
- 2   Tbsp. cornstarch
- 1   Tbsp. lemon juice
- 1   tsp. grated lemon zest
- ½   tsp. ground cinnamon
- 1   package (8 oz.) refrigerator crescent rolls
   Ground cinnamon (to sprinkle over top before baking)
   Sugar (to sprinkle over top before baking)

COBBLERS & CRISPS

Preheat oven to 400 degrees.

In an 8-inch square glass-baking dish, toss blueberries, sugar, cornstarch, lemon juice and zest, and cinnamon until combined.

Microwave on high for 3 minutes at a time, stirring twice, for a total of 6 to 7 minutes, until mixture thickens.

Unroll crescent rolls on a floured cutting board. Press perforations together to form an eight-inch square piece.

Place on top of blueberry mixture.

Sprinkle top with cinnamon and sugar.

Bake at 400 degrees for about 12 minutes or until golden brown.

Cool before serving.

Makes 4 to 6 servings.

Blueberry Gobbler

Your family and friends will be sure to gobble this one up.

Blueberry Mixture
- 6 cups blueberries, rinsed and well-drained
- ¼ cup sugar
- 2 Tbsp. cornstarch

Topping
- 1⅓ cups all-purpose flour
- 2 Tbsp. sugar
- ¾ tsp. baking powder
- ¼ tsp. baking soda
- ⅛ tsp. salt
- 5 Tbsp. chilled butter, cut into small pieces
- 1 cup plain yogurt
- 2 Tbsp. skim milk
- 1½ tsp. sugar (to sprinkle over top of dough)

Preheat oven to 350 degrees.

Grease a 9-inch square baking pan.

Blueberry Mixture
Combine blueberry mixture ingredients in a bowl. Pour into greased baking pan. Set aside.

Topping
In a large bowl whisk flour, sugar, baking powder, baking soda, and salt. Using a pastry cutter, cut in butter until mixture forms crumbs. Stir in yogurt to form a soft dough.

Evenly spoon dough over blueberry mixture to form 9 dumplings. Brush each dumpling with milk. Finish with sprinkles of sugar.

Bake at 350 degrees for 50 to 55 minutes or until dumplings are golden. Juice from the berries will be bubbly around the dumplings.

Makes 9 servings.

Dorthy's Blueberry "Something"

Blueberry Mixture
- 5 cups blueberries, fresh or frozen
- 1 cup sugar
- ¼ cup all-purpose flour

Topping
- 2½ cups all-purpose flour
- 1 tsp. baking powder
- 1 cup Crisco®
- ¼ cup (½ stick) chilled butter, cut into small pieces
- ¼ cup sugar
- 1 cup milk

Finish
- 1 Tbsp. butter
- ½ Tbsp. sugar

Preheat oven to 350 degrees.

Blueberry Mixture
Butter a 13- x 9- x 2-inch glass oven-proof baking dish.
Evenly place blueberries on the bottom of dish.
Sprinkle sugar over the blueberries. Then sprinkle the
flour. Set aside.

Topping
In a large bowl combine flour and baking powder. With
a fork mix in Crisco® and butter until mixture forms
crumbs. Add sugar and milk. Stir until combined.

Spoon topping over blueberry mixture.

Finish
Dot with butter. Sprinkle sugar over the top.

Bake at 350 degrees for 55 to 60 minutes or until
lightly brown.

Makes 8 to 10 servings.

Granny's Blueberry Surprise

- 4 cups Granny Smith apples, peeled and coarsely chopped (3 to 4 apples)
- 3 cups blueberries
- 2 Tbsp. brown sugar
- 1 Tbsp. cornstarch
- 1 cup *less* 2 Tbsp. all-purpose flour
- ¾ cup sugar
- 1 tsp. baking powder
- ½ tsp. ground cinnamon
- ¼ tsp. ground nutmeg
- ⅛ tsp. salt
- 1 large egg, beaten
- ½ cup (¼ stick) butter, melted

Preheat oven to 350 degrees.

Butter the bottom and sides of a 13- x 9- x 2-inch glass oven-proof baking dish.

Line bottom of buttered dish with apples. Top with blueberries.

Mix brown sugar with cornstarch. Sprinkle over fruit.

In a large bowl combine flour, sugar, baking powder, cinnamon, nutmeg, and salt. With a fork, stir in egg until mixture is crumbly. Sprinkle over fruit. Drizzle melted butter over top.

Bake at 350 degrees for about 55 minutes or until top is golden and juice from the berries bubbles through.

Cool on a wire rack for 15 minutes. Serve warm or cold.

Makes 8 servings.

Quick and Easy Crisp

4 cups blueberries
⅓ cup sugar
⅓ cup all-purpose flour
¾ cup rolled oats
⅓ cup brown sugar
¼ cup (½ stick) chilled butter, cut into
    small pieces

Preheat oven to 350 degrees.

Generously grease a 9-inch square baking pan.

In a bowl gently toss blueberries with sugar.

Line bottom of greased pan with blueberries.

In a large bowl whisk flour, oats, and brown sugar. Using a pastry cutter, cut in butter until mixture forms crumbs. Sprinkle over blueberries.

Bake at 350 degrees for 30 to 35 minutes.

Makes 6 servings.

True Blue Crisp

Topping
- 1 cup all-purpose flour
- 1 cup rolled oats
- ½ cup sugar
- ½ cup chopped walnuts
- 1 tsp. ground cinnamon
- ⅛ tsp. salt
- ½ cup (1 stick) chilled butter, cut into small pieces

Filling
- 6 cups blueberries
- 1 cup *Topping*

Preheat oven to 375 degrees.

Butter the bottom and sides of a 13- x 9- x 2-inch glass oven-proof baking dish.

Topping
In a large bowl whisk flour, oats, sugar, chopped walnuts, cinnamon, and salt. Using a pastry cutter, cut in butter until mixture forms crumbs. Measure one cup of topping (to be combined with blueberries).

Filling
Combine blueberries and one cup of topping in a separate large bowl. Spread filling evenly on bottom of buttered dish. Cover with remaining topping.

Bake at 375 degrees for 45 minutes.

Cool slightly on a wire rack. Serve warm.

Makes 8 to 10 servings.

Pies

Barbara's No-Bake Pie

1 package (8 oz.) cream cheese, softened
2 Tbsp. confectioners' sugar
1 Tbsp. cold milk
2 Tbsp. graham cracker crumbs
4 cups blueberries, washed and dried on
      paper towels
1 jar (6 oz.) blueberry jam
One 9-inch baked graham pie shell

In a large bowl, with mixer at medium speed, beat cream cheese until creamy. Add confectioners' sugar and cold milk. Continue to beat until mixture is smooth and fluffy.

Sprinkle graham cracker crumbs on baked graham pie shell.

Pour cream cheese mixture.

Cover with blueberries.

In a saucepan, heat the blueberry jam until smooth.

Spoon over pie.

Chill at least 3 hours or until set.

Makes 8 servings.

Blueberry Yogurt Pie

2   containers (8 oz.) vanilla yogurt
2   cups blueberries, washed and drained
1   container (8 oz.) Cool Whip®
One   9-inch baked graham pie crust

Place yogurt in a large bowl.

Fold in blueberries, then Cool Whip®.

Evenly spread mixture into baked graham pie crust.

Cover and freeze for at least 4 hours.

Let stand at room temperature for 30 minutes before serving.

Store leftovers, if any, in freezer.

Makes 8 servings.

Cranberry and Blueberry Chocolate Pie

Ted Murphy, chef at the Mountaineer Inn

Crust
        Pastry for a single-crust pie
  3 Tbsp. sugar

Filling
  1 cup whole cranberries
  1 cup blueberries
  ½ cup sugar
  ½ cup cold cranberry juice
  1 Tbsp. cornstarch
  1½ cups chocolate chips
  1 cup chopped cranberries (raw)

Topping
  ½ cup chocolate chips, melted

Preheat oven to 375 degrees.

Crust
Pastry line a 10-inch pie plate. Prick bottom and sides with fork. Sprinkle sugar on top of entire crust.

Bake crust at 375 degrees for 10 minutes, until crust is caramelized.

Cool on a wire rack.

Filling
In a 2-quart saucepan combine whole cranberries, blueberries, and sugar. Dissolve cornstarch in cold cranberry juice. Add to saucepan.

Cook and stir over medium-high heat until mixture begins to boil. Continue to boil and stir for 4 to 5 minutes, until mixture thickens. Remove from stove and set aside.

Cover the caramelized (bottom) crust with chocolate chips. Follow with chopped cranberries.

Cover chopped cranberries with cooked berries. Drizzle melted chocolate (or your favorite chocolate sauce) over top.

Bake at 375 degrees for 20 to 25 minutes or until crust turns brown and flakes.

Serve with vanilla ice cream.

Makes 8 to 10 servings.

Granny's Blueberry Pie

Apple Mixture
- 2 Tbsp. (¼ stick) butter
- 2 Granny Smith apples, peeled and sliced
- 2 Tbsp. sugar
- ⅛ tsp. salt

- 3 cups blueberries, rinsed and well-drained
- 2 Tbsp. sugar
     Pastry for a double-crust pie

In a 3-quart saucepan melt butter. Add apples, sugar, and salt. Stir gently over medium-high heat until apples are tender (about 6 to 7 minutes) and most of the liquid is absorbed by the apples.

Let stand to cool about 30 minutes.

Preheat oven to 425 degrees.

Pastry-line a 9-inch glass pie plate. Add blueberries. Sprinkle sugar over the berries.

Spread apple mixture evenly over the top.

Place top crust over fruit filling. Seal and flute the edge. Cut slits in the top crust.

Bake at 425 degrees for 30 to 35 minutes (cover edge of crust with strips of foil after the first 10 to 15 minutes of baking) or until the top is golden brown.

Cool on a wire rack.

Makes 8 servings.

Sally's Open Blueberry Pie

4 cups blueberries, washed and divided
¼ cup water
1 cup sugar
3 Tbsp. cornstarch
¼ tsp. salt
1 tsp. butter
1 tsp. lemon juice
One 10-inch baked pie shell

Pour 2 cups of blueberries into the baked pie shell.

In a saucepan combine the remaining 2 cups of blueberries and water. Cook and stir over medium-high heat.

When mixture begins to boil, add sugar, cornstarch, and salt. Continue to boil and stir until mixture thickens (to the consistency of jam).

Remove from heat. Stir in butter and lemon juice.

Pour the cooked blueberry mixture over the fresh blueberries.

Allow to set.

When ready to serve, top with whipped cream or ice cream.

Makes 8 servings.

Spicy Blueberry Pie

- ¾ cup sugar
- 3 Tbsp. cornstarch
- ½ tsp. ground cinnamon
- ¼ tsp. ground nutmeg
- ⅛ tsp. salt
- 4 cups blueberries
- 1 Tbsp. butter
  Pastry for a double-crust pie

Preheat oven to 425 degrees.

Pastry line a 9-inch glass pie plate.

In a large bowl combine sugar, cornstarch, cinnamon, nutmeg, and salt. Add blueberries. Toss gently until blueberries are covered. Pour into the lined pie plate.

Dot with butter.

Place top crust over fruit filling. Seal and flute the edge. Cut slits in the top crust.

Bake at 425 degrees for about 35 to 40 minutes (cover edge of crust with strips of foil after the first 10 to 15 minutes of baking) or until top is golden. Juice from the berries will start to bubble over the crust.

Cool on a wire rack.

Makes 8 servings.

Sweet B&B Pie

4	cups blueberries, divided
1	cup sugar
¼	cup water
3	Tbsp. cornstarch
1	tsp. lemon juice
2	large bananas, cut into small pieces
One	9-inch baked graham pie crust

In a medium saucepan combine 2 cups blueberries, sugar, water, cornstarch, and lemon juice. Cook over medium-high heat stirring constantly. Bring to a full boil.

Continue to boil and stir for about one minute until mixture thickens to the consistency of jam.

Remove from heat. Stir in the remaining 2 cups of blueberries. Set aside.

Evenly arrange banana pieces over the bottom of pie crust.

Pour blueberry mixture over the banana pieces.

Cover and refrigerate over night.

Serve with vanilla ice cream.

Makes 8 to 10 servings.

Wild Blueberry Pie

¾ cup sugar
2 Tbsp. all-purpose flour
4 cups wild blueberries
¼ tsp. ground nutmeg
¼ tsp. ground cinnamon
1 Tbsp. butter
   Pastry for a double-crust pie

PIES

Preheat oven to 425 degrees.

Pastry line a 9-inch glass pie plate.

In a small bowl mix sugar and flour. Spread one-fourth of mixture on the lined pie plate.

Fill with blueberries.

Sprinkle remaining mixture over blueberries.

Sprinkle nutmeg and cinnamon. Dot with butter.

Place top crust over fruit filling. Seal and flute the edge. Cut slits in the top crust.

Bake at 425 degrees for 30 to 35 minutes (cover edge of crust with strips of foil after the first 10 to 15 minutes of baking) or until top is golden. Juice from the berries will start to bubble over the crust.

Cool on a wire rack.

Makes 8 servings.

Cookies & Sweets

Blueberry Butter Cookies

½ cup (1 stick) butter, softened
½ cup confectioners' sugar
½ tsp. vanilla extract
¾ cup all-purpose flour
1 Tbsp. cornstarch
⅛ tsp. salt
½ cup dried wild blueberries

Preheat oven to 350 degrees.

Grease cookie sheet.

In a large bowl, with mixer at low speed, cream butter, confectioners' sugar, and vanilla until smooth and fluffy.

In a separate bowl sift together flour, cornstarch, and salt. .

Add sifted ingredients and dried wild blueberries to creamed mixture. Blend well by hand until dough forms a ball.

Shape small amounts of dough into one-inch balls.

Place one inch apart on greased cookie sheet; flatten slightly.

Bake at 350 degrees for 10 to 12 minutes.

Immediately remove from cookie sheet.

Makes 2 dozen.

Kisses for Kids

1   chilled bowl and beaters

2   large egg whites, room temperature
½   cup sugar
1   tsp. vanilla extract
¾   cup dried wild blueberries

Preheat oven to 250 degrees.

Line cookie sheet with aluminum foil.

Beat egg whites until very stiff. Add sugar, one tablespoon at a time, beating after each addition. Continue to beat until meringue forms stiff peaks. Then beat in vanilla.

Fold in dried blueberries.

Drop the meringue from a teaspoon onto the aluminum foil.

Bake at 250 degrees for 50 to 55 minutes or until kisses can be easily lifted from the cookie sheet.

When done, turn oven setting to "off" and leave oven door open. Allow kisses to dry in the oven for 2 to 3 hours.

Makes 2 dozen.

Fudge for the Fourth

1 package (8 oz.) cream cheese, softened
4 cups confectioners' sugar
1 tsp. vanilla extract
1 package (12 oz.) white chocolate, melted
1 cup dried cranberries
1 cup dried wild blueberries

Butter a 9-inch square baking pan.

In a large bowl beat cream cheese, confectioners' sugar, and vanilla until smooth and fluffy.

Gradually add melted chocolate. Continue to beat until well blended.

Stir in dried fruits.

Spread fudge into buttered baking pan.

Cover and refrigerate overnight.

Makes 3 dozen.

Special Feature

Meet Kristine Hastreiter

Kristine specializes in handmade preserves, biscotti, and chocolates, as well as artisan breads and "made-from-scratch" cakes, cookies and confections. She began making preserves and biscotti as a hobby using family  recipes. Initially, she gave gourmet baskets filled with jars of jam, biscotti, and chocolates as holiday gifts to family members, friends, and colleagues.

Frustrated by the scarcity of artistic opportunities in her professional field, Kristine took a sabbatical to explore her culinary talents. In the summer of 2003, she started making the rounds at local craft fairs and farmers markets. Soon she had a dedicated following purchasing her culinary creations.

In the fall of 2004, Kristine decided to pursue her dream of opening a gourmet pastry shop. She enrolled in Culinary School and began refining her recipes, including the following ones that are easy. Kristine hopes to open her pastry shop in the Wareham area in the near future.

"Kristine's Culinary Creations"

Fruit Chutney

In India the word "chutney" denotes both a slow-cooked preserve and a mixture made of finely chopped raw (uncooked) ingredients. Chutneys (whether cooked or uncooked) contain chopped fruit or vegetables preserved with sugar, spices and vinegar, and are typically seasoned with garlic, onion, and ginger.

Blueberries, apples and cranberries give this chutney a real fruit flavor. Serve as an accompaniment to roast beef, beef tenderloin, prime rib, or roast pork.

3	cups blueberries, fresh or frozen
1½	cups apples, peeled, cored, chopped (3 medium apples)
1	cup cranberries, fresh or frozen
¾	cup onion, chopped (1 medium onion)
½	cup white vinegar or cider vinegar
½	cup orange juice
½	cup granulated sugar
½	cup brown sugar
1	Tbsp. fresh orange zest
½	tsp. salt
½	tsp. garlic powder
¼	tsp. ground ginger
⅛	tsp. cayenne pepper (optional!)

"KRISTINE'S CULINARY CREATIONS"

Place all ingredients in a non-reactive saucepan.

Bring to a boil over medium heat, continually stirring. Cook until mixture has thickened to a jam-like consistency, about 20 to 30 minutes (apples and onions will be soft and translucent).

Ladle into sterilized jars, leaving a ¼-inch headspace.

Adjust two-piece caps.

Process 15 minutes in a boiling water canner.

Yield: Four 8 oz. jars.

Chutney can also be placed in a plastic container and kept in the refrigerator.

Recipe can be doubled or tripled if a larger amount of chutney is desired.

Reduced Sugar Apple Blueberry Jam

This is a fantastic, luscious jam, which can be used in a variety of ways. It is a great garnish for baked Brie cheese, a topping for ice cream or cheesecake, and a wonderful addition to a trifle.

Because blueberries and apples are high in natural pectin, the jam is made without commercial pectin (Sure-Jell® or Certo®). This allows the amount of sugar to be reduced without compromising the blueberrylicious flavor!

    3   cups apples, peeled, cored, chopped
          (MacIntosh, Cortland, or Empire apples
          work best.)
    3   cups blueberries, fresh or frozen
    ½   cup Splenda®
    ½   cup granulated sugar
    ¼   cup water
    1   Tbsp. lemon juice or white vinegar
    ⅛   tsp. salt (optional)

Place all ingredients in a non-reactive saucepan.

Bring to a boil over medium heat, continually stirring. Cook until mixture has thickened and apples are soft and translucent.

Ladle into sterilized jars, leaving a ¼-inch headspace.

Adjust two-piece caps.

Process 15 minutes in a boiling water canner.

Yield: Three 8 oz. jars.

Jam can also be placed in a plastic container and kept in the refrigerator.

Recipe can be doubled or tripled if a larger amount of jam is desired.

Chocolate Blueberry Truffles

These delicious fruity chocolate truffles make a great gift, or a delightful end to a meal served with coffee or a glass of chocolate liqueur.

¼   cup heavy cream (or half-and-half)
8   oz. semi-sweet chocolate morsels
3   Tbsp. unsalted butter, room temperature
½   cup dried blueberries, finely chopped
    Unsweetened cocoa for dusting

In a small saucepan bring cream to a simmer. Remove from heat.

Stir in chocolate and butter. If chocolate does not completely melt, place the pan in hot water (double boil method), and continue to stir mixture until all the chocolate morsels have melted.

Add chopped dried blueberries. Mix until combined.

Transfer chocolate blueberry mixture to a shallow bowl.

Cool, cover and refrigerate overnight, until firm.

"Kristine's Culinary Creations"

Place unsweetened cocoa in a pie plate.

Line a baking sheet with wax paper.

Dip melon baller, small spoon, or scoop into a glass of warm water. Shake off excess water and quickly scrape across surface of chilled truffle mixture to form a rough one-inch ball. Place in cocoa.

Gently shake pie plate to coat truffles evenly with the cocoa. Place truffles on the baking sheet.

Continue scooping out truffles and coating them with cocoa powder until all the chocolate blueberry truffle mixture is gone.

Store truffles in a wax-paper-lined container, separating each layer with wax paper.

Cover tightly and keep in the refrigerator or freeze.

Yield: Approximately 3 dozen truffles.

About the Author

YOLANDA **L**ODI loves to experiment in creating unique dishes to satisfy her taste and to share with family and friends. She is the author of two previous cookbooks. *Yolanda's Cranberry Country Recipes* is an eclectic collection of many traditional and original recipes from Cranberry Country. *Yolanda's Hand-Me-Down Recipes* captures the rich cultural heritage of cooking in New England. Compiling these books brought so much enjoyment to her and everyone who contributed that she started collecting recipes for a much needed all-blueberry cookbook.

Yolanda hopes that this cookbook will inspire others to compile and preserve their own special recipes.

She lives in southeastern Massachusetts with her husband, Ed, her greatest fan and taste tester.